José Maréchal
Photography by Akiko Ida

verrines

starters and sweets in small glasses

MURDOCH BOOKS

contents

tips

A verrine – pronounced *vair-een*, from the French word for glass (*verre*) – is an entrée or a dessert interestingly composed with layers of food of different texture, flavour and colour.

Whether they are savoury or sweet, cold or warm, sophisticated or casual, verrines seem to have captured the creativity and imagination of Parisian cooks, and are now making their way around the world.

The tools
There are several methods of carefully creating each successive layer of your verrines, depending on the consistency of the ingredients. A piping bag is ideal for mousse, cream, vegetable caviar, taramasalata, tapenade and other fairly soft ingredients. For stiffer ingredients, such as grains, chopped fruit or vegetables, use a small teaspoon or a long (parfait) spoon, depending on the width and height of the glass. Finally, for liquid ingredients, such as pesto or pistou sauce, fromage blanc, syrup or crème anglaise, a baster will be more precise and easier to handle than a spoon.

Verrine glasses
You may already have an assortment of shot glasses, Champagne flutes, tumblers, martini glasses, espresso cups, or custard bowls that can be used as verrines. For recipes requiring cooking in an oven, ensure that the glasses are heatproof. If you don't have enough glasses, an inexpensive solution is to buy plastic disposable glasses, wine glasses, or small sauce containers which will do the job very well.

The guide to number of serves is based on: small 60-80 ml (2-2½ fl oz) glasses, medium 100-125 ml (3½-4 fl oz) glasses, large 200-250 ml (7-9 fl oz) glasses.

Shaping biscuits
To shape biscuits or make circles the same diameter as the verrine glass, use a biscuit cutter or, even better, the upturned verrine glass; all you do is press down on the biscuit dough while gently twisting.

Verrines in a flash
You don't need to be a great chef or spend a lot of time in the kitchen to make verrines that are original and tasty. There are some great ideas for quick and easy savoury verrines on pages 60-63 and sweet verrines on pages 122-125.

To make different layers, all you need are ready-made sweet or savoury biscuits for crumbling. Garnish your verrines with crackers, grissini, pain d'épice, speculaas (spice) biscuits, Breton shortbreads, rolled wafers . . . the choices are endless.

Think ahead
Prepare ahead of time for your party: use ice-cube or silicon trays to make frozen portions of dips such as pesto, tapenade, coulis and mousse. Then tip them out when you're ready to add the final ingredients to make your verrines.

Decorated verrines
For cocktails, have elegant 'rimmed' verrines in a flash. Lightly moisten the edge of the glass with a syrup or fruit juice, then dip it in caster, crystal or raw sugar for sweet, and egg white and salt or chopped herbs for savoury.

Express granitas
How about adding a sugar syrup to Champagne, muscat, puréed fruit or vegetables for a sparkling and very summery verrine! Pour the prepared mixture into a wide, shallow container and place it in the freezer for at least 3 hours, stirring from time to time with a fork or a small whisk, working from the edges towards the centre to make lovely ice crystals.

savoury

Niçoise crumble with goat's cheese cream

Makes 4-6 large glasses

CRUMBLE TOPPING

100 g (3½ oz) soft unsalted butter

200 g (7 oz/1⅔ cups) plain (all-purpose) flour

1 egg yolk, lightly beaten

RATATOUILLE

150 ml (5 fl oz) olive oil

1 large eggplant (aubergine), finely diced

2 zucchini (courgettes), finely diced

1 red capsicum (pepper), finely diced

1 onion, finely chopped

2 garlic cloves, finely chopped

1 sprig each thyme and rosemary

3 tomatoes, peeled, seeded and finely diced

GOAT'S CHEESE CREAM

100 ml (3½ fl oz) pouring cream

120 g (4¼ oz) fresh goat's cheese

2 tablespoons olive oil

To make the crumble topping, use your fingertips to rub together the butter, flour and a pinch of salt until the mixture resembles coarse breadcrumbs. Mix through the egg with a flat-blade knife until the mixture forms small lumps. Refrigerate for 15 minutes.

Meanwhile, to make the ratatouille, heat 2 tablespoons of the olive oil in a large frying pan. Cook the eggplant over high heat for 8-10 minutes until golden and tender, then tip into a strainer placed over a bowl. Add another 2 tablespoons of the oil and cook the zucchini. Repeat with the capsicum.

In the same pan, heat the remaining oil and cook the onion, garlic, thyme and rosemary until soft. Return the drained vegetables to the pan, add the tomato, season and cook for a further 1-2 minutes over low heat. Allow to cool.

Preheat the oven to 180°C (350°F/Gas 4).

To make the goat's cheese cream, warm the cream in a saucepan over low heat. Crumble the goat's cheese into a mixing bowl and gradually pour in the cream while stirring with a wooden spoon. Mix in the olive oil and season with salt and pepper.

Scatter the crumble mixture on a baking tray and bake for 10-12 minutes, or until golden.

To assemble the verrines, remove the thyme and rosemary from the ratatouille, then arrange a layer of the ratatouille in the bottom of the glasses. Add the goat's cheese cream using a piping bag or small spoon, then top with the crumble.

Butterfly pasta with vegetables

Makes 8-12 medium glasses

250 g (9 oz) farfalle (butterfly pasta)

100 ml olive oil

20 g (¾ oz/⅓ cup) basil leaves

1 garlic clove, peeled

1 tablespoon pine nuts, plus extra roasted nuts, to sprinkle

1 zucchini (courgette), sliced into rounds

1 small eggplant (aubergine), finely diced

250 g (9 oz) cherry tomatoes, halved

juice of 1 lemon

Cook the pasta in boiling salted water with a dash of the olive oil until *al dente*. Drain and refresh under cold water.

Meanwhile, to make the pesto, pound the basil, garlic, pine nuts and a little of the olive oil with a mortar and pestle. Set aside in the refrigerator.

Heat 1½ tablespoons of the olive oil in a frying pan. Add the zucchini and eggplant, season to taste, and toss over high heat for 4-5 minutes, or until tender.

Put the vegetables in a large bowl. Add the pasta, pesto, cherry tomatoes and lemon juice and combine well. Add some more olive oil and adjust the seasoning if necessary, then cover and refrigerate for about 30 minutes, or until the pasta salad is quite cold.

To assemble the verrines, divide the pasta salad evenly among the glasses. Sprinkle with some roasted pine nuts just before serving.

Laughing Cow cheese, ham and cucumber

Makes 4-6 small glasses

12 portions (1½ packets)
Laughing Cow cheese or
210 g (7½ oz) cheese spread

3-4 slices ham, finely diced

1 Lebanese (short)
cucumber, halved
lengthways, seeded
and finely diced

Put the cheese into a small bowl and beat until smooth.

To assemble the verrines, arrange alternate layers of ham, cucumber and cheese in the glasses.

TIP You can use prawns (shrimp) or smoked salmon in place of ham.

Sicilian-style penne with tuna

Makes 8–12 medium glasses

250 g (9 oz) penne pasta

80 g (2¾ oz) pitted black olives, finely chopped

80 g (2¾ oz/½ cup) sun-dried tomatoes in oil, drained and finely chopped

150 g (5½ oz) tinned tuna in water or brine, drained and flaked

olive oil, for drizzling

balsamic vinegar, for drizzling

Cook the pasta in boiling salted water with a dash of olive oil until *al dente*. Drain and refresh under cold water.

Put the olives, sun-dried tomatoes, tuna and pasta in a bowl. Drizzle with olive oil and balsamic vinegar, and season to taste, then combine well. Cover the bowl with plastic wrap and refrigerate for at least 30 minutes, or until ready to serve.

To assemble the verrines, divide the tuna pasta salad evenly among the glasses. Serve the verrines chilled, offering additional olive oil and balsamic vinegar on the side.

Goat's cheese, dried fruit and sun-dried tomatoes

Makes 4-6 large glasses

120 g (4¼ oz) sun-dried tomatoes in oil, drained

50 g (1¾ oz) dried apricots, finely chopped

50 g (1¾ oz) prunes, pitted and finely chopped

50 g (1¾ oz) dried figs, finely chopped

250 g (9 oz) fresh goat's cheese

150 ml (5 fl oz) pouring cream

50 ml (1½ fl oz) olive oil

wild rocket (arugula) leaves, to serve

grissini, to serve

Place the sun-dried tomatoes in a food processor and process until smooth.

Mix the dried fruit together and place in a bowl.

Crumble the goat's cheese into a separate bowl. Gently heat the cream in a saucepan over low heat, then add the cheese and olive oil and mix until smooth. Season to taste.

To assemble the verrines, start with a layer of the cheese mixture. Add a layer of tomato, a second layer of cheese, a layer of fruit and top with a final layer of the cheese.

Serve with a few wild rocket leaves and a grissini stick.

Watermelon gazpacho

Makes 6-8 medium glasses

¼ small watermelon, flesh removed, seeded and coarsely chopped

2 tomatoes, seeded and coarsely chopped

½ red capsicum (pepper), seeded and coarsely chopped

½ red onion, coarsely chopped

2 tablespoons olive oil

125 ml (4 fl oz/½ cup) canned tomato juice

2 drops grenadine

sliced watermelon, to garnish (optional)

Put all of the ingredients in a food processor and blend until smooth. Strain if necessary to obtain a smooth gazpacho. Season and refrigerate for at least 1 hour.

To serve, fill the verrine glasses with gazpacho and garnish with small slices of watermelon, if desired.

SAVOURY | preparation + cooking time: 20 minutes

Boudin noir, speculaas and spiced banana

Makes 4-6 medium glasses

2 boudin noir (blood sausages)

2 bananas

30 g (1 oz) lightly salted butter

2 pinches curry powder

2 pinches ground ginger

2 pinches ras el hanout spice mix

1 teaspoon soft brown sugar

4 speculaas (spice) biscuits, finely crushed

Peel the sausages, crumble the meat using a fork and cook in a non-stick frying pan over low heat for 2-3 minutes, stirring constantly. Use a spoon to arrange the sausage meat in the bottom of the verrine glasses.

Cut the bananas into thick slices without peeling them. Melt the butter in a frying pan over medium heat, add the spices and brown sugar, and brown the rounds of banana for 1 minute on each side.

Sprinkle the crushed speculaas over the meat and finish with the spiced banana. Serve immediately.

Avocado–orange milkshake with crab

Makes 6–8 medium glasses

1 ripe avocado, peeled
and stone removed

1 tablespoon caster
(superfine) sugar

juice of 2 oranges

100 ml (3½ fl oz) milk

200 g (7 oz) crabmeat,
flaked

Process the avocado, sugar and orange juice in a food processor. Add the milk, a little at a time, blending well until the mixture is smooth. Transfer to an airtight container and refrigerate for at least 1 hour.

To assemble the verrines, stir the crabmeat through the chilled milkshake, then divide evenly among the glasses.

TIP You can adjust the sweetness and consistency of the milkshake by altering the amount of sugar and liquid used. For a more savoury milkshake, season lightly with salt and pepper.

Scallops with boudin noir and green apple

Makes 4–6 small glasses

2 green apples
(such as granny smith),
peeled and cored

10 g (¼ oz) lightly salted
butter

1 tablespoon soft brown
sugar

2 boudin noir (blood
sausages)

4–6 large scallops

1 tablespoon olive oil

sea salt

thin slices unpeeled apple,
to serve

Slice the apples into small segments. In a saucepan, melt the butter over low heat, add the apple and sugar, cover and cook over very low heat for 5–6 minutes, stirring occasionally until tender.

Peel the sausages, crumble the meat with a fork and cook in a non-stick frying pan over low heat for 2–3 minutes, stirring constantly. Use a spoon to arrange the sausage meat in the bottom of the glasses, then add the cooked apple.

Just before serving, pan-fry the scallops in very hot olive oil for 1 minute on each side. Place a scallop on each verrine. Season with a pinch of sea salt and top with a slice of apple. Serve immediately.

TIP If you like, add a pinch of sichuan pepper when cooking the apples.

Mini vegetable verrines

Makes 15–18 small glasses

CUMIN-SPICED CARROT

1 large carrot, peeled and chopped

1 teaspoon roasted cumin seeds

MINTED ZUCCHINI

1 large zucchini (courgette), finely diced

3 tablespoons finely shredded mint

SPINACH WITH NUTMEG

200 g (7 oz) frozen chopped spinach, thawed

1 scant teaspoon freshly ground nutmeg

4 eggs

200 ml (7 fl oz) pouring cream

100 ml (3½ fl oz) milk

For the cumin-spiced carrot, cook the carrot in boiling salted water until tender. Refresh under running water and set aside.

For the minted zucchini, divide the zucchini and mint among one-third of the heatproof glasses.

For the spinach with nutmeg, squeeze the thawed spinach between your hands to remove all excess moisture. Divide the spinach and ground nutmeg among another one-third of glasses.

Preheat the oven temperature to 160ºC (315ºF/Gas 2–3).

Put the eggs, cream and milk in a bowl, season to taste, and whisk until well combined. Pour two-thirds of the egg mixture evenly among the zucchini and spinach glasses.

Process the remaining egg mixture and carrot in a food processor until smooth. Pour into the remaining glasses and sprinkle with the cumin seeds.

Place the verrines in a deep roasting tin filled two-thirds with hot water, then place in the oven to cook for about 15 minutes, or until just set. Serve warm.

Mixed melon balls with port and prosciutto grissini

Makes 6 large glasses

50 g (1¾ oz) caster (superfine) sugar

250 ml (9 fl oz/1 cup) ruby or tawny port

1 rockmelon or any orange-fleshed melon

¼ watermelon

6 thin slices prosciutto

1 packet grissini

50 g (1¾ oz) soft lightly salted butter

Heat the sugar and port in a small saucepan over low heat, stirring until the sugar dissolves, then simmer until reduced by half. Allow to cool.

Make the melon balls using a melon-baller (small cubes will also work).

Cut each slice of prosciutto lengthways into three strips. Brush half the length of the grissini with the softened butter, then roll the strips of prosciutto around them. Refrigerate for 10 minutes.

To assemble the verrines, divide the melon balls among the glasses. To serve, add the grissini, then pour over the port syrup.

TIP The grissini absorb moisture from the fruit and port and can break: wait until the last minute to arrange them in the glasses or serve them on the side.

Spanish rice

Makes 8-12 medium glasses

4 tablespoons olive oil

1 onion, finely chopped

1 red capsicum (pepper), finely diced

pinch of saffron

250 g (9 oz) medium-grain rice

1 small bouquet garni (or 1 chicken or vegetable stock cube)

125 g (4½ oz) chorizo sausage, finely diced

155 g (4½ oz/1 cup) frozen peas

Heat the olive oil in a heavy-based saucepan and cook the onion over medium heat for 6-8 minutes or until slightly coloured. Add the capsicum and saffron, and cook for 1 minute, stirring constantly.

Add the rice and bouquet garni (or crumbled stock cube). Stir for 1-2 minutes, then add 600 ml (21 fl oz) of water. Reduce the heat to low and simmer, uncovered, until all the liquid has been absorbed.

About 5 minutes before the rice has finished cooking, stir in the sausage and peas. Remove from the heat and allow to cool. Season to taste.

To assemble the verrines, divide the Spanish rice evenly among the glasses.

TIP Top with extra slices of chorizo if desired.

Mimosa egg

Makes 4-6 small glasses

6 eggs

250 g (9 oz/1 cup)
whole-egg mayonnaise

Place the eggs in a large saucepan and cover with cold water. Bring the water to the boil, then boil the eggs for 5 minutes. Drain, then cool under running water. Peel the eggs, then separate the whites from the yolks.

Push the whites through a sieve or fine strainer and place in a bowl. In a separate bowl, mash the yolks using a fork. Add half the mayonnaise to each bowl and combine until creamy. Season with salt and pepper.

To assemble the verrines, use a piping bag or small spoon to layer the egg white and yolk.

TIP You can vary this simple recipe by adding fresh herbs or spices to the egg yolk.

Maki-verrine

Makes 6-8 small glasses

120 g (4¼ oz) Japanese sushi rice

1 tablespoon rice vinegar

2 teaspoons caster (superfine) sugar

large pinch salt

3 sheets nori seaweed

120 g (4¼ oz) skinless salmon fillet, thinly sliced

120 g (4¼ oz) bluefin tuna, thinly sliced

wasabi, to serve

6–8 slices pickled ginger, to serve

soy sauce, to serve

Rince the rice under cold water, then drain. Place in a small saucepan with 180 ml (6 fl oz/¾ cup) of water and bring to the boil, stirring occasionally. Cover, then reduce the heat to low and cook for 10 minutes. Remove from the heat and stand, covered, for 10 minutes.

Meanwhile, combine the vinegar, sugar and salt in a small saucepan and heat gently, stirring until the sugar has dissolved. Pour the vinegar mixture over the cooked rice and combine very gently. Allow to cool.

Place the nori sheets, smooth side up, on a clean board. Use one of the verrine glasses to trace out circles with the point of the knife, then cut them out with scissors.

To assemble the verrines, arrange alternate layers of nori circles, rice, salmon and tuna.

Serve the verrines topped with a very small dollop of wasabi and a slice of pickled ginger, with soy sauce passed around separately.

Macaroni, lamb's lettuce, Roquefort and pear

Makes 4–6 large glasses

POACHED PEARS

3 pears (such as williams or conference)

zest of 1 lemon

100 g (3½ oz/⅔ cup) elbow macaroni

80 g (2¾ oz) Roquefort cheese, crumbled

1 head lamb's lettuce (corn salad), leaves picked

100 ml (3½ fl oz) olive oil

50 ml (1½ fl oz) balsamic vinegar

Bring a large saucepan of water to the boil. Peel the pears, leaving the stalks intact. Add the pears and lemon zest to the boiling water and reduce to medium heat. Cover and cook the pears for 20 minutes or until they are tender, turning them occasionally. Remove the pears with a slotted spoon and drain.

Allow the pears to cool, then cut off the top third of the pears, then slice the tops lengthways to form six pear garnishes. Set aside until needed.

Meanwhile, cook the macaroni in boiling salted water with a dash of olive oil until *al dente*. Drain and refresh under cold water.

Finely dice the remaining pear flesh, discarding the core. Combine the diced pear, cheese, lettuce and macaroni in a bowl.

Whisk the olive oil and balsamic vinegar together to make a vinaigrette dressing. Season to taste.

To assemble the verrines, divide the macaroni salad among the glasses, decorate with a pear top, then drizzle with a little dressing just before serving.

Prawns, petit salad and mayonnaise

Makes 6-8 medium glasses

1 egg yolk, at room temperature

juice of 1 lemon

230 ml (7¾ fl oz) olive oil

18–24 baby English spinach leaves

30 g (1 oz/⅓ cup) mung bean shoots or alfalfa sprouts

12–16 large raw prawns (shrimp), peeled with tails intact

To make the mayonnaise, whisk the egg yolk and lemon juice in a small bowl, then gradually add 165 ml (5½ fl oz/⅔ cup) of the olive oil. Season with salt and pepper and refrigerate for 10 minutes.

Mix together the spinach leaves and bean sprouts in a separate bowl and set to one side.

Heat 1½ tablespoons of the olive oil in a large frying pan. Cook half the prawns over high heat for 2 minutes or until just cooked, then drain on paper towels. Repeat the process with the remaining oil and prawns.

To assemble the verrines, put a spoonful of lemon mayonnaise in the bottom of each glass. Divide the prawns and petit salad among the glasses. Serve immediately.

Trio of foie gras and fruit

Makes 12 small glasses

PEAR COMPOTE

2 pears, peeled and cored

1 tablespoon honey

3 pinches ground cinnamon

APRICOT COMPOTE

250 g (9 oz) fresh apricots, stones removed

70 g (2½ oz) soft brown sugar

juice of ½ lemon

3 pinches ground ginger

FIG COMPOTE

200 g (7 oz) fresh figs

70 g (2½ oz) soft brown sugar

½ sprig rosemary

50 ml (1½ fl oz) port

250 g (9 oz) foie gras, thinly sliced

grissini, to serve

sea salt, to serve

To make the fruit compotes, use three small saucepans.

Chop each fruit into large dice and put in individual saucepans. Cook the fruit, sugar or honey and appropriate spice for each compote over low heat for 7–8 minutes, stirring regularly until softened.

Remove from the heat, allow to cool, then transfer into separate containers and refrigerate for 1 hour.

To assemble the verrines, spoon a quarter of one of the compotes among four glasses. Repeat with the other compotes for the remaining glasses. Top each verrine with a small slice of foie gras, then serve with grissini and sea salt.

TIPS Buy a good sausage-shaped foie gras so you can make nice round slices.

You could also serve small slices of toasted fruit bread with the verrines.

Zucchini caviar with parmesan cream

Makes 6-8 small glasses

2 large zucchini
(courgettes), sliced into
rounds

2 pinches ground cumin

1 sprig rosemary

1 garlic clove, crushed

1 tablespoon olive oil

100 g (3½ oz/1 cup) grated
parmesan cheese

200 ml (7 fl oz) pouring
cream

shaved parmesan, to
garnish

ground black pepper, to
garnish

Cook the zucchini in boiling salted water for 2 minutes, then refresh in cold water. Mash lightly with a fork, then stir in the cumin, rosemary sprig, garlic and olive oil. Season to taste. Cook the zucchini mixture in a saucepan over low heat for 2-3 minutes to allow the flavours to infuse. Remove from the heat. Remove the rosemary and allow the zucchini caviar to cool in the refrigerator for 30 minutes.

Meanwhile, heat the parmesan cheese and cream in a small saucepan over low heat, stirring constantly until the cheese has melted and the cream is reduced without the mixture sticking. Remove from the heat and transfer to another container and allow to cool.

To assemble the verrines, divide the zucchini caviar evenly among the glasses to two-thirds full.

Before serving, reheat the cream to just lukewarm and carefully pour it over the verrines. Decorate with a shaving of parmesan and a sprinkle of ground pepper.

Eggplant caviar, ricotta and coppa

Makes 4-6 large glasses

2 large eggplants
(aubergines), halved
lengthways

2 onions, chopped

5 garlic cloves, chopped

3 tablespoons olive oil

1 teaspoon thyme

1 teaspoon tomato paste
(concentrated purée)

150 g (5½ oz) ricotta cheese

5–6 slices coppa

Preheat the oven to 200°C (400°F/Gas 6).

Score the inside flesh of the eggplants with a knife, then arrange them in an ovenproof dish. Scatter the onion and garlic over the eggplant, then drizzle with 2 tablespoons of the olive oil. Season with salt and pepper, add the thyme leaves, then bake for 25 minutes, or until the eggplant is soft. Remove from the oven and allow to cool.

Once cooled, use a tablespoon to scoop out the eggplant flesh. Process the eggplant flesh, onion, garlic, tomato paste and remaining olive oil in a food processor until smooth. Refrigerate for 45 minutes.

Beat the ricotta with an electric mixer until smooth.

To assemble the verrines, use a piping bag or small spoon to layer the eggplant caviar in the glasses. Add the ricotta over the eggplant, then top with the coppa, either arranged into a rosette shape or cut into thin strips.

Salmon tartare, green apple and redcurrants

Makes 6-8 medium glasses

400 g (14 oz) skinless salmon fillet, finely diced

1 green apple (such as granny smith), peeled, cored and finely diced

3 tablespoons lemon juice

3 tablespoons olive oil

1 French shallot, finely chopped

1 small punnet redcurrants

Combine the salmon and apple in a bowl. Add the lemon juice and olive oil and mix well. Add the shallot and redcurrants and combine. Season to taste.

To assemble the verrines, divide the combined mixture evenly among the glasses. Refrigerate the verrines for at least 20 minutes before serving.

Lemony quinoa, rocket pesto and salmon roe

Makes 6 medium, or
12 small glasses

100 g (3½ oz/½ cup) quinoa

50 ml (1½ fl oz) lemon juice

3 tablespoons olive oil

150 g (5½ oz) salmon roe

60 g (2¼ oz/¼ cup) sour cream

ROCKET PESTO

40 g (1½ oz/2 cups loosely packed) rocket (arugula)

50 g (1¾ oz/1 cup) basil

2 garlic cloves, peeled

2 tablespoons finely grated parmesan cheese

1½ tablespoons pine nuts or almonds

75 ml (2¼ fl oz) olive oil

Place the quinoa in a saucepan with 150 ml (5 fl oz) of cold water and a pinch of salt and pepper. Bring to the boil over high heat, then cover. Reduce the heat to low and cook for 15 minutes, or until the water has been absorbed. Add the lemon juice and olive oil, and season to taste. Remove from the heat and allow to cool, stirring from time to time.

To make the rocket pesto, place the rocket, basil, garlic, parmesan cheese and pine nuts or almonds in a food processor and process while gradually adding the olive oil. Season to taste and refrigerate for 20 minutes.

To assemble the verrines, alternate layers of quinoa, pesto and salmon roe, varying the combination depending on the size of the glass. To serve, add a small spoonful of sour cream.

Bacon–celeriac milkshake

Makes 6-8 small glasses

¼ bulb celeriac, peeled and finely diced

400 ml (14 fl oz) milk

6 slices bacon, 4 chopped, the rest cut into pieces

2 tablespoons olive oil

grissini, to serve

Put the celeriac, milk, 4 roughly chopped bacon and a pinch of salt and pepper into a saucepan and cook over medium heat until the celeriac is tender. Process the cooked mixture in a food processor, adjusting the consistency and seasoning if necessary, then transfer to an airtight container. Cool, then refrigerate for 2 hours.

Heat the oil in a non-stick frying pan and cook the remaining bacon over medium heat until golden and crisp. Drain on paper towels.

To assemble the verrines, divide the celeriac mixture evenly among the glasses, then garnish the verrines with pieces of crispy bacon. Serve with grissini.

Italiano

Makes 4-6 medium glasses

60 g (2¼ oz) sun-dried tomatoes in oil, drained

4 small vine-ripened tomatoes, peeled, seeded and finely diced

1–2 balls fresh buffalo mozzarella cheese

60 g (2¼ oz) black olive tapenade

50 g (1¾ oz) ready-made pesto

grissini, to serve

Process the sun-dried tomatoes in a food processor and combine with the diced fresh tomatoes.

Cut the mozzarella into thin slices and, using a biscuit cutter or an upturned glass, cut out circles the diameter of the verrine glasses.

To assemble the verrines, arrange a layer of the tapenade, then the mozzarella, the tomatoes, another layer of mozzarella, then a top layer of pesto. Serve with a few grissini on the side.

Fresh goat's cheese, green apple and smoked duck breast

Makes 4-6 medium glasses

2 green apples (such as granny smith), peeled, cored and sliced into small segments

80 ml (2¾ fl oz/⅓ cup) pouring (whipping) cream

2 small, round fresh goat's cheeses (crottins)

2 tablespoons olive oil

8–12 thin slices smoked duck breast

Place the apple in a heavy-based saucepan with 2 tablespoons of water. Cover and simmer over low heat for 6-8 minutes, or until tender. Cool, then refrigerate for 15 minutes.

Heat the cream in a small saucepan over low heat until lukewarm. Season with salt and pepper.

Crumble the goat's cheese into a small bowl. Gradually pour the warm cream over mashing the cheese with a fork. Add the olive oil and stir until smooth.

To assemble the verrines, put a small spoonful of goat's cheese cream in the bottom of each glass. Add a layer of apple and top with slices of smoked duck breast.

Tapioca with smoked salmon and avocado

Makes 8–10 small glasses

80 g (2¾ oz) pearl tapioca

3 tablespoons olive oil

juice of 1 lemon

2 avocados, peeled and stones removed

½ teaspoon ground cumin

6 slices smoked salmon, finely chopped

Bring 1 litre (35 fl oz/4 cups) of lightly salted water to the boil. Add the tapioca and cook over medium heat for 15 minutes, stirring regularly, until translucent. Drain, rinse under cold running water, then place the tapioca in a bowl with the oil and half the lemon juice. Season to taste and combine well. Refrigerate until needed.

Process the avocado, the remaining lemon juice and the cumin in a food processor until smooth, add salt and pepper to taste.

To assemble the verrines, fill a piping bag with the avocado. Alternate layers of avocado, smoked salmon and tapioca, or mix the tapioca with the salmon and just have two layers. Chill for 30 minutes. Serve very cold.

Cherry chutney with Manchego cheese

Makes 6-8 small glasses

300 g (10½ oz) pitted fresh cherries

60 g (2¼ oz) caster (superfine) sugar

½ teaspoon ground ginger

2 pinches ground cinnamon

3 tablespoons white wine vinegar

100 g (3½ oz) Manchego (sheep's milk) cheese, shaved or finely diced

To make the chutney, put the cherries and sugar in a non-stick saucepan and cook gently over medium heat, stirring constantly, until the sugar has dissolved. Add the ginger, cinnamon and a pinch of freshly gound pepper, and simmer for 2-3 minutes. Add the vinegar and cook for a further few minutes, stirring gently, until the mixture reaches a compote-like consistency. Remove from the heat. Transfer the cherry mixture to an airtight container, cool, then refrigerate for at least 30 minutes before serving.

To assemble the verrines, divide the chutney evenly among the glasses. Top with manchego cheese before serving.

TIP You can also use fresh goat's cheese or blue cheese with a chutney of cherries or other seasonal fruits.

Savoury verrines in a flash . . .

Vegetable gazpacho with frozen fruit blocks

Make ice blocks using fruit juice or coulis and add a fruity touch to vegetable juice: try carrot/pineapple; capsicum (pepper)/raspberry; beetroot (beet)/orange; cucumber/ strawberry.

Duo of taramasalatas and crackers

Combine different taramasalatas (cod, salmon) in successive layers and serve with pieces of cracker for added crunch.

Boursin, tomatoes and tapenade

Mash Boursin cheese in a bowl until smooth, finely dice tomatoes, then make up the verrines along with some black olive tapenade, playing with the combination of colours.

Cucumber, fromage blanc and mint

For a pleasant, light summer verrine, layer small cubes of cucumber with creamy fromage blanc and fresh mint. Serve well chilled.

Seafood sticks, tzatziki and peanuts

A creamy and crunchy verrine that's very simple to make. Top flaked seafood or crab sticks with tzatziki and crushed peanuts, and enjoy.

Feta and olives with tomato-basil coulis

Simply combine cubes of marinated feta cheese with flavoured olives, then thin out a tomato-basil sauce with a little water and pour over the verrines just before serving.

Hummus with carrot purée and tacos

Hummus, the smooth Lebanese purée of chickpeas, served with a sweet carrot purée and topped with spicy corn chips, will delight your guests.

Prawns with St-Môret cheese, curry and mango

How about a touch of the exotic? Serve a few shelled prawns (shrimp), some creamy St-Môret cheese, a few small cubes of mango and a dusting of Indian curry powder.

Fromage blanc with lumpfish roe

Layers of fromage blanc or cream cheese with red and black lumpfish roe.

Tartare-style cubes of beef

A classic but still delicious. Leave it plain or serve with capers, mustard and other condiments.

Large prawns with spices

Cooked and shelled, large prawns (shrimp) can also be marinated in a drizzle of olive oil flavoured with a mixture of curry, paprika, turmeric, or other spices (the list is endless) . . . a guaranteed taste trip!

Mozzarella, marinated prosciutto and sun-dried tomato

This classic trio of Italian flavours makes for an elegant antipasto-inspired verrine . . . Simply skewer the mozzarella and tomato on a toothpick, and wrap in prosciutto.

Tomato, avocado and orange

A light verrine for a summer buffet: a fresh and fruity mixture of finely diced tomato, avocado and orange, seasoned with a drizzle of lemon and a few drops of olive oil.

Potatoes and smoked fish

Haddock, trout and mackerel bought smoked and marinated with herbs, berries or various condiments, can be stylishly beached on a few cubes of lukewarm boiled potato. Add a dollop of crème fraîche to finish.

Poached egg with salmon roe

A poached egg (cooked in 1 minute – simplicity itself!) served with orange-hued salmon roe and a scattering of chopped chives takes on a more chic aspect.

Ham and gouda, *à la parisienne*

Cubes of ham and gouda cheese . . . the crème fraîche and chives are almost superfluous! And so a verrine replaces the baguette to convey a timeless classic.

Scallops with vanilla oil

Add a split vanilla bean and some salt and pepper to some olive oil and marinate scallops for 30 minutes. Then briefly pan-fry them and serve straight away.

Smoked duck breast and artichoke hearts with balsamic vinegar

Thin slices of smoked duck breast prettily wrapped around marinated artichoke hearts and secured with a skewer, then drizzled with balsamic vinegar.

sweet

Tiramisu

Makes 6-8 large glasses

500 ml (17 fl oz/2 cups) lukewarm espresso coffee

150 g (5½ oz/⅔ cup) caster (superfine) sugar

18–24 savoiardi (sponge fingers)

100 ml (3½ fl oz) amaretto liqueur

3 eggs, separated

250 g (9 oz) mascarpone cheese

3 tablespoons unsweetened cocoa powder, to serve

Pour the coffee into a bowl, add 100 g (3½ oz) of the sugar and mix well until the sugar has dissolved. Dip the biscuits in the sweetened coffee and press them down into the base of the glasses (three per glass). Use your fingertips to make a well-soaked and even layer, and drizzle with amaretto to taste. Place the glasses in the refrigerator.

Whisk the egg yolks with 1½ tablespoons of the sugar until the mixture becomes thick and pale. Beat in the mascarpone until smooth.

Whisk the egg whites until soft peaks form, add the remaining sugar and beat until stiff peaks form. Using a spatula, carefully fold the beaten egg whites into the mascarpone mixture.

Fill the glasses with the cream and refrigerate for at least 2 hours. Dust verrines with cocoa powder before serving.

Panna cotta with mixed berries

Makes 6-8 medium glasses

300 ml (10½ fl oz) milk

300 ml (10½ fl oz) pouring cream

120 g (4¼ oz) caster (superfine) sugar

1 vanilla bean, split lengthways

4 small gelatine leaves

2 tablespoons soft brown sugar

200 g (7 oz) mixed berries (fresh, or frozen and thawed)

Place the milk, cream and caster sugar in a heavy-based saucepan, scrape in the vanilla seeds and stir over low heat until the sugar has dissolved, then simmer for 5 minutes.

Soak the gelatine in cold water until soft, then drain and squeeze out the excess water.

Remove the cream mixture from the heat and stir in the gelatine until it has dissolved, then divide the mixture among the glasses. Place the verrines in the refrigerator for 2 hours.

Meanwhile, dissolve the brown sugar with a little water in a saucepan over low heat, then add the berries. Simmer gently for 1-2 minutes. Remove from the heat and allow to cool.

Spoon the berries over each verrine just before serving.

Rice pudding, raspberries and speculaas

Makes 6-8 large glasses

RICE PUDDING

250 ml (9 fl oz/1 cup) milk

150 ml (5 fl oz) pouring cream

60 g (2¼ oz/¼ cup) caster (superfine) sugar

90 g (3¼ oz) short-grain rice

1 vanilla bean, split lengthways

2 small gelatine leaves

250 g (9 oz/2 cups) raspberries

60 g (2¼ oz/¼ cup) caster (superfine) sugar

6 speculaas (spice) biscuits

To make the rice pudding, heat the milk, cream and sugar in a heavy-based saucepan over medium heat. Rinse the rice in cold water and add to the milk mixture along with the vanilla bean just before it comes to the boil. Reduce the heat to low and cook, stirring regularly, until the rice is tender. Allow to cool. Remove the vanilla bean then refrigerate the pudding for at least 45 minutes.

Meanwhile, soak the gelatine leaves in cold water until soft, then squeeze out the excess water. Place the raspberries, sugar and 2 tablespoons of water in a saucepan. Warm slightly over low heat until the sugar dissolves, then add the gelatine and stir until it dissolves. Cool, then refrigerate until cold.

Crush the speculaas biscuits in a food processor or with a rolling pin until they resemble fine breadcrumbs.

To assemble the verrines, arrange a layer of rice pudding in each glass, then a layer of raspberries, and finish with the crushed speculaas.

Coconut–lime verrines

Makes 6-8 medium glasses

2 whole eggs

2 egg yolks

200 ml (7 fl oz) sweetened condensed milk

200 ml (7 fl oz) coconut milk

100 g (3½ oz) desiccated coconut

zest and juice of 1 lime

thick cream, to serve

Preheat the oven to 160ºC (315ºF/Gas 2-3).

Place the eggs, egg yolks, condensed milk, coconut milk, dessicated coconut, lime juice and one-quarter of the lime zest in a bowl and whisk until well combined.

Fill the heatproof glasses with the mixture. Place them in a deep roasting tin, then pour in enough hot water to come halfway up the side of the glasses. Cook for 15-20 minutes, or until just set but still a little wobbly. Remove from the water bath. Allow to cool at room temperature, then refrigerate for at least 1 hour before serving.

To serve, decorate with a spoonful of cream and sprinkle with remaining lime zest.

Strawberry muesli with mascarpone

Makes 6-8 large glasses

250 g (9 oz) mascarpone
cheese

50 g (1¾ oz) fromage blanc
or ricotta cheese

70 g (2½ oz) icing
(confectioners') sugar,
plus extra for dusting

300 g (10½ oz) strawberries,
hulled and diced

150 ml (5 fl oz) ready-made
strawberry coulis, or
puréed strawberries

75 g (2½ oz) muesli with
dried fruit

Place the mascarpone, fromage blanc or ricotta and the icing sugar in a bowl and whisk together until smooth.

Combine the strawberry pieces with the coulis and divide evenly among the glasses. Top with the mascarpone cream, then refrigerate for 20 minutes.

To serve, top the verrines with the muesli and dust with a little icing sugar.

Vanilla-honey pineapple confit with mascarpone cream

Makes 6-8 medium glasses

2 tablespoons honey

1 large pineapple, peeled and chopped into small cubes

1 vanilla bean, split lengthways

MASCARPONE CREAM

2 egg yolks

1 tablespoon vanilla sugar

250 g (9 oz) mascarpone cheese

To make the confit, heat the honey in a non-stick frying pan over high heat for 2 minutes, then add the pineapple. Scrape the vanilla seeds into the pan and cook for 7–8 minutes, stirring occasionally, until the pineapple takes a caramel colour. Remove from the heat and allow to cool.

To make the mascarpone cream, place the egg yolks and sugar in a bowl and whisk until thick and pale. Add the mascarpone cheese and beat until smooth.

To assemble the verrines, divide the mascarpone cream evenly among the glasses, then top with the confit. Serve immediately.

Summer crumble with apples and mixed berries

Makes 6-8 large glasses

60 g (2¼ oz) unsalted butter

120 g (4¼ oz/⅔ cup lightly packed) soft brown sugar

6 golden delicious apples, peeled, cored and chopped into large pieces

70 g (2½ oz) caster (superfine) sugar

125 g (4½ oz/1 cup) raspberries

60 g (2¼ oz) blackberries

60 g (2¼ oz) bilberries or blueberries

juice of 1 lemon

CRUMBLE TOPPING

50 g (1¾ oz) plain (all-purpose) flour

50 g (1¾ oz/¼ cup lightly packed) soft brown sugar

50 g (1¾ oz/½ cup) ground almonds

½ teaspoon ground cinnamon

60 g (2¼ oz) soft, lightly salted butter

Melt the butter and brown sugar in a saucepan. Add the apple pieces, stir and cook gently over low heat, covered, for 10 minutes. Remove from the heat, allow to cool, then refrigerate for 10 minutes.

To make the crumble topping, combine all of the dry ingredients in a bowl, then rub in the butter using your fingertips until the mixture resembles coarse breadcrumbs. Refrigerate for 15 minutes.

Preheat the oven to 180°C (350°F/Gas 4).

Meanwhile, place the caster sugar, mixed berries and lemon juice in a saucepan and cook over low heat for 2-3 minutes, stirring occasionally. Remove from the heat and set aside.

Spread the crumble mixture on a baking tray and bake for 10-12 minutes, or until golden.

To assemble the verrines, spoon alternate layers of apple and berries in the glass, or mix the apples and berries together. Finish by topping each verrine with the crumble.

Bilberries with red wine and rosemary

Makes 6-8 medium glasses

750 ml (26 fl oz/3 cups) red wine

100 g (3½ oz) caster (superfine) sugar

400 g (14 oz) bilberries or blueberries

2 sprigs rosemary

Place the red wine and sugar in a saucepan and stir over medium heat until the sugar dissolves, then simmer for 10-15 minutes, until the mixture has reduced by half. Add the berries and rosemary and simmer for another 2-3 minutes, then remove from the heat.

Remove the rosemary and reserve for serving. Allow the berries to cool in the syrup and then refrigerate for 45 minutes, or until chilled.

To assemble the verrines, fill the glasses with berries and a little wine syrup and garnish with rosemary.

Irish chocolate–coffee

Makes 8 large glasses

125 ml (4 fl oz/½ cup) milk

4 egg yolks

125 g (4½ oz) caster (superfine) sugar

5 small gelatine leaves

1 tablespoon natural coffee extract

100 ml (3½ fl oz) whiskey

200 g (7 oz) dark chocolate

750 ml (26 fl oz/3 cups) whipping cream

chocolate-covered coffee beans (optional) or instant coffee, to serve

Place the milk in a saucepan and bring to just below the boil.

Meanwhile, whisk the egg yolks and sugar together in a large heatproof bowl until thick and pale. Pour the hot milk into the egg mixture, stirring continuously, until well combined.

Return the milk mixture to the same saucepan and stir over low heat until the mixture thickens enough to coat the back of a wooden spoon. (Do not allow the mixture to boil.) Remove from the heat and pour into the heatproof bowl.

Soak the gelatine leaves in cold water until soft, then drain and squeeze out the excess water. Add the gelatine to the hot custard and stir until dissolved. Add the coffee extract and whiskey and allow to cool to room temperature.

Put the chocolate in another heatproof bowl over a saucepan of boiled water, making sure the base of the bowl does not touch the water. Allow to stand until the chocolate has melted. Use a large spatula to spread the chocolate thinly over a large baking tray lined with baking paper. Refrigerate until nearly set. Using a biscuit cutter the same diameter as the base of the verrine glass mark out 20 circles. Refrigerate until completely set.

Whisk 500 ml (17 fl oz/2 cups) of the cream until soft peaks form and fold into the coffee-whiskey mousse.

To assemble the verrines, arrange two alternate layers of the mousse and chocolate discs for each glass. Refrigerate for at least 1½ hours before serving.

To serve, whip the remaining cream and spoon over the top of the verrines. Sprinkle with chocolate-coated coffee beans or instant coffee to decorate.

Brioche pudding with citrus fruits

Makes 6-8 large glasses

3 oranges

2 grapefruit

4 small brioche

2 eggs

60 g (2¼ oz) caster
(superfine) sugar

1 tablespoon cornflour
(cornstarch)

150 ml (5 fl oz) milk

100 ml (3½ fl oz) pouring
cream

Preheat the oven to 160ºC (315ºF/Gas 2-3).

Remove the skin and pith of the oranges and grapefruit with a small sharp knife, reserving all the juice from both fruit.

Cut the brioche into 1 cm (½ inch) thick slices, the same diameter as the verrine glasses.

Beat the eggs and sugar together using electric beaters until pale and fluffy.

Combine the cornflour with 2 tablespoons of the milk in a small bowl to make a thin paste. Add to the egg mixture, together with the cream and remaining milk, and whisk until well combined.

To assemble the verrines, place a slice of brioche in the bottom of each heatproof glass, then layer with citrus fruit and moisten with a little juice. Continue alternating layers of brioche and fruit in the glasses until three-quarters full. Pour the custard mixture over the verrines, in two stages, so that it seeps right down to the bottom of each glass.

Place the verrines in a deep roasting tin half-filled with water and bake for about 20 minutes, or until just set. Allow to cool, then refrigerate for at least 1 hour. This verrine is best enjoyed quite cold.

TIP You can add a dash of Grand Marnier or Cointreau to the citrus juice soaked up by the slices of brioche.

Mini crème brûlée

Makes 12-16 small glasses

375 ml (13 fl oz/1½ cups) pouring cream

125 ml (4 fl oz/½ cup) milk

4 egg yolks

60 g (2¼ oz) caster (superfine) sugar

2 teaspoons natural vanilla extract

2 teaspoons natural coffee extract

2 teaspoons unsweetened cocoa powder

½ teaspoon natural pistachio or almond extract

120 g (4¼ oz) raw sugar

handheld cook's blowtorch for caramelising

Preheat the oven to 90ºC (190ºF/Gas ½).

Place the the cream and milk in a saucepan and bring to the boil over medium-low heat. Whisk the egg yolks and caster sugar together in a bowl until well combined, then pour over the boiling milk mixture and stir to combine.

Divide the mixture among four bowls, then add one of the four flavours to each bowl and stir well. Fill the heatproof glasses with different custards.

Place the glasses in a deep roasting tin, then fill with enough hot water to come halfway up the sides of the glasses. Bake for 1-1½ hours, depending on the size of the glasses, then refrigerate for at least 2 hours.

To serve, sprinkle raw sugar over the top of each verrine and caramelise using a cook's blowtorch. Be careful when you do this, so that you don't break the glass.

TIP Make sure that the oven temperature does not go above 100ºC (200ºF/Gas ½).

Peach in green tea jelly

Makes 8 large glasses

4 peaches

100 g (3½ oz) caster (superfine) sugar

25 g (1 oz/⅓ cup) green tea leaves, tied in a piece of muslin (cheesecloth)

6 small gelatine leaves

Blanch the peaches in a saucepan of boiling water for 10 seconds. Drain, peel, halve and remove the stones.

Place the sugar and 750 ml (26 fl oz/3 cups) of water in a large saucepan and stir over low heat until the sugar has dissolved, then bring to the boil. Add the peaches and muslin bag of green tea and simmer for 5 minutes.

Meanwhile, soak the gelatine in cold water until soft, then drain and squeeze out the excess water.

Remove the saucepan from the heat. Transfer the peaches to a bowl and allow to cool, then refrigerate.

Remove the muslin bag from the syrup. Strain the syrup through a fine sieve into another heatproof bowl, then dissolve the gelatine in the syrup.

To assemble the verrines, pour about 2 cm (¾ inch) of syrup into the bottom of each glass and place in the refrigerator for at least 1 hour. Allow the remaining syrup to stand at room temperature. Once the jelly has set, place a peach half in each glass and pour in the remaining green tea syrup. Return the verrines to the refrigerator for another hour, or until the jelly has set. Serve chilled.

Strawberries with basil and limoncello

Makes 6-8 large glasses

50 g (1¾ oz) caster (superfine) sugar

150 ml (5 fl oz) limoncello liqueur

500 g (1 lb 2 oz) strawberries, hulled and diced

40 g (1½ oz/⅔ cup) finely shredded basil

Place the sugar and 200 ml (7 fl oz) of water in a small saucepan and simmer over low heat for 5 minutes, stirring until the sugar has dissolved. Remove from the heat, add the limoncello and allow to cool.

Mix half the strawberries and the shredded basil in a bowl, then divide among the glasses. Pour the limoncello syrup over the top of each verrine, then chill them in the refrigerator for 15 minutes.

Serve chilled garnished with the remaining shredded basil.

Apricot mousse with ginger

Makes 6-8 large glasses

300 g (10½ oz) apricots in syrup, drained

50 g (1¾ oz) caster (superfine) sugar

20 g (¾ oz) glacé ginger, plus extra to decorate

1 teaspoon ground ginger

5 small gelatine leaves

300 ml (10½ fl oz) whipping cream

6 slices pain d'épice or gingerbread, finely diced

To make the coulis, process the apricots, sugar and the glacé and ground ginger in a food processor. Keep 125 ml (4 fl oz/ ½ cup) of the apricot-ginger coulis aside in the refrigerator for serving, then pour half the remaining coulis mixture into a saucepan and warm over low heat.

Meanwhile, soak the gelatine in cold water until soft. Drain, then squeeze out the excess liquid. Add the gelatine to the warm coulis and stir until dissolved. Remove from the heat, then add the remaining coulis and combine well. Allow to cool.

Whip the cream in a large bowl until firm peaks form. Gently fold into the coulis to make apricot mousse.

To assemble the verrines, divide the pain d'épice among the glasses. Top with the apricot mousse and refrigerate for at least 2 hours.

To serve, pour a little of the chilled reserved coulis over each verrine and decorate with a slice of glacé ginger.

Banana tatin, palmito biscuits and crème épaisse

Makes 6-8 medium glasses

200 g (7 oz) caster (superfine) sugar

4 bananas, peeled and sliced into thick rounds

50 g (1¾ oz) unsalted butter

1 packet of palmito (palmier) biscuits

200 ml (7 fl oz) sour cream

Scatter the sugar over the base of a frying pan, sprinkle with 1 tablespoon of water and shake the pan over low heat until you obtain a light caramel. Add the bananas and butter, then cook for 2-3 minutes, turning to coat bananas. Remove from the pan and allow to cool.

To assemble the verrines, arrange the cooled bananas and sour cream in alternating layers, separating each layer with a palmito biscuit. Serve immediately.

TIP You can give a Caribbean touch to this recipe by adding a dash of rum and some raisins to the bananas.

Fresh grapefruit marmalade

Makes 6-8 medium glasses

8 grapefruit

3 tablespoons honey

yoghurt or ice cream, to serve

Remove the skin and pith of the grapefruit with a small sharp knife. Then remove the segments, reserving all the juice.

Place the honey in a frying pan and warm over medium heat for 2 minutes. Add the grapefruit segments and juice, simmer while stirring for 2 minutes, or until just warm. Remove from the heat and allow to cool. Transfer the grapefruit marmalade to an airtight container and refrigerate for at least 20 minutes.

To serve, place a scoop of vanilla ice cream or yoghurt in each glass, then top with the marmalade.

TIPS This is also a great accompaniment to a chocolate dessert. If desired, add a little ginger, cinnamon or vanilla.

Apples with honey and pain d'épice

Makes 6-8 small glasses

4 tablespoons honey

4 green apples (such as granny smith), peeled, cored and chopped into wedges

40 g (1½ oz) unsalted butter

6 slices pain d'épice or gingerbread, diced

icing (confectioners') sugar, for dusting

Place the honey in a frying pan and cook over low heat until lightly caramelised. Add the apple and butter, and increase the heat to medium. Stir for 6-8 minutes, or until the apple mixture is tender. Allow to cool.

To assemble the verrines, divide the apple evenly among the glasses, then top with pain d'épice.

Dust with icing sugar and serve immediately.

Chocolate custard with frosted fruit

Makes 6-8 medium glasses

250 ml (9 fl oz/1 cup) milk

250 ml (9 fl oz/1 cup) pouring cream

6 egg yolks

90 g (3¼ oz) caster (superfine) sugar

3 tablespoons unsweetened cocoa powder

2 bananas, peeled and sliced into small pieces

2 pears, peeled and sliced into small pieces

125 g (4½ oz/1 cup) raspberries

Heat the milk and cream over medium heat until just below boiling. Remove from the heat.

Whisk the egg yolks and sugar in a heatproof bowl until the mixture becomes thick and pale. Add the cocoa and combine well. Pour the hot milk mixture over the egg mixture and combine well. Return the custard mixture to the saucepan, and stir constantly with a wooden spoon over low heat for 3-4 minutes, until the mixture thickens enough to coat the back of the spoon. Remove from the heat and allow to cool. Divide the custard among the glasses, then refrigerate for 1 hour.

Meanwhile, to make the frosted fruit, place the bananas, pears and raspberries in a single layer on a tray and freeze for about 45 minutes before serving.

To assemble the verrines, top the chocolate custard with the frosted fruit and serve immediately.

Délice du Café Noir

Makes 8-10 long glasses

CHOCOLATE-CARAMEL MOUSSE

50 g (1¾ oz) caster
(superfine) sugar

250 ml (9 fl oz/1 cup)
pouring cream

120 g (4¼ oz) dark
chocolate, chopped

3 egg yolks

1 tablespoon icing
(confectioners') sugar

WHITE CHOCOLATE MOUSSE

1 small gelatine leaf

250 ml (9 fl oz/1 cup)
whipping cream

150 g (5½ oz) white
chocolate, chopped

150 ml (5 fl oz) dark
chocolate sauce

To make the chocolate-caramel mousse, place the caster sugar in a small saucepan and shake over low-medium heat until it caramelises. Add 85 ml (2¾ fl oz) of the cream and stir until the mixture dissolves. Place the chocolate pieces in a heatproof bowl, pour the caramel cream over and stir until the chocolate is melted and smooth. Add the egg yolks and combine.

In a separate bowl, whisk the remaining cream with the icing sugar until soft peaks form, then gently fold into the chocolate-caramel mixture. Divide the chocolate-caramel evenly among the glasses, so that it fills one-third of each glass, then place in the refrigerator for 30 minutes.

To make the white chocolate mousse, soak the gelatine in cold water until soft, then drain and squeeze out the excess water.

Meanwhile, pour 125 ml (4 fl oz/½ cup) of the cream into a small saucepan and bring to the boil. Remove from the heat. Add the gelatine and stir until smooth. Place the white chocolate in a heatproof bowl, pour the cream mixture over and stir until the chocolate is melted and smooth, then stand until cool.

In a separate bowl, whisk the remaining cream until soft peaks form, then gently fold into the white chocolate mixture.

Remove the glasses from the refrigerator. Divide the white chocolate among the verrines so that it fills up to the two-third mark of each glass. Return to the refrigerator for another 30 minutes.

Finish assembling the verrines by topping with chocolate sauce and refrigerate until ready to serve.

Chocolate mousse surprise

Makes 6-8 medium glasses

150 ml (5 fl oz) ready-made
raspberry coulis

150 ml (5 fl oz) ready-made
apricot coulis

150 ml (5 fl oz) ready-made
kiwifruit coulis

CHOCOLATE MOUSSE

125 g (4½ oz) dark
chocolate, chopped

30 g (1 oz) unsalted butter

30 g (1 oz) crème fraîche

2 egg yolks

4 egg whites

1 scant tablespoon icing
(confectioners') sugar

Pour the different coulis into separate ice block trays or sachets and place in the freezer for 2 hours, or until frozen. (Don't make the fruit blocks too large; they should be no larger than the diameter of the glass.)

To make the chocolate mousse, place the chocolate and butter in a heatproof bowl over a saucepan of boiled water, making sure the base of the bowl does not touch the water. Allow to stand until the chocolate and butter have melted. Mix in the crème fraîche, then the egg yolks, and stir until smooth.

In a separate bowl, whisk the egg whites until soft peaks form, then add the sugar and whisk until stiff peaks form. Fold into the chocolate mixture and refrigerate until it is just set.

To assemble the verrines, fill a piping bag with the mousse as soon as it is set. Place a fruit block in the bottom of each glass, then add some mousse. Alternate layers of mousse and coulis blocks, then place the verrines in the refrigerator for at least 1½ hours. As the blocks gently melt, the different coulis colours will be pressed between the layers of mousse.

Tropical trifle with coconut tapioca

Makes 8-10 medium glasses

COCONUT TAPIOCA

250 ml (9 fl oz/1 cup) milk

500 ml (17 fl oz/2 cups) coconut milk

70 g (2½ oz) caster (superfine) sugar

110 g (3¾ oz) pearl tapioca

CRUMBLE TOPPING

2 tablespoons plain (all-purpose) flour

1½ tablespoons soft brown sugar

2 tablespoons ground almonds

2 tablespoons desiccated coconut

30 g (1 oz) soft, lightly salted butter

125 g (4 oz/⅔ cup lightly packed) soft brown sugar

1 pineapple, peeled and diced into large cubes

2 mangoes, peeled and diced into large cubes

2 scoops passionfruit sorbet

4 small gelatine leaves

pulp of 3 passionfruit

To make the coconut tapioca, heat the milk, coconut milk and caster sugar in a saucepan over medium heat to just below boiling point. Add the tapioca and cook over low heat, stirring constantly, for 15 minutes, or until the tapioca is translucent. Allow to cool.

To make the crumble topping, place all the dry ingredients in a bowl, then rub in the butter using your fingertips until the mixture resembles breadcrumbs. Place the crumble mixture in the refrigerator for 15 minutes.

Preheat the oven to 180°C (350°F/Gas 4).

Heat the brown sugar in a large frying pan over medium heat. Add the pineapple and cook for 2-3 minutes, stirring to coat. Add the mango and the passionfruit sorbet and cook for a further 1-2 minutes, then remove from the heat.

Soak the gelatine in cold water until soft, then drain and squeeze out the excess water. Add the gelatine and passionfruit pulp to the pan. Allow to cool.

Meanwhile, spread the crumble mixture onto a baking tray and bake for 10-12 minutes, or until golden. Remove from the oven and break up with a fork.

To assemble the verrines, divide the fruit mixture among the glasses, then top with the coconut tapioca. Before serving, sprinkle the crumble mixture over the verrines.

TIP You can serve a raspberry coulis on the side with this verrine.

Raspberries melba

Makes 6-8 medium glasses

400 ml (14 fl oz) pouring (whipping) cream

2 tablespoons icing (confectioners') sugar

½ vanilla bean

250 g (9 oz/2 cups) raspberries

1 litre (35 fl oz/4 cups) raspberry sorbet

400 ml (14 fl oz) ready-made raspberry coulis

40 g (1½ oz) flaked toasted almonds, to decorate (optional)

To make the chantilly cream, place the cream and icing sugar into a bowl. Split the vanilla bean lengthways and scrape the seeds into the cream. Whip the cream using an electric beater until firm peaks form, then refrigerate for 10 minutes.

To assemble the verrines, place a few raspberries in the bottom of each glass (reserving some for garnish), then top with a scoop of sorbet. Pour a little coulis over the sorbet.

Fill a piping bag fitted with a fluted nozzle with the chantilly cream and decorate the verrines. Drizzle with a little remaining coulis, top with a raspberry and a few toasted almonds and serve immediately.

Shortbread biscuits with lemon curd and ginger

Makes 8 medium glasses

SHORTBREAD

125 g (4½ oz) soft unsalted butter

90 g (3¼ oz/½ cup) caster (superfine) sugar

3 egg yolks

150 g (5½ oz/1 cup) plain (all-purpose) flour

½ teaspoon baking powder

LEMON CURD

3 whole eggs

6 egg yolks

75 g (2¾ oz) caster (superfine) sugar

125 ml (4 fl oz/½ cup) strained lemon juice

110 g (3¾ oz) cold unsalted butter

110 g (3¾ oz) white chocolate, chopped

40 g (1½ oz) glacé ginger, roughly chopped, to garnish

To make the shortbread pastry, beat the butter and sugar with electric beaters until pale and fluffy. Add the egg yolks and combine well. Stir in the flour, baking powder and a pinch of salt and combine just until the dough comes together. Shape the dough into a disc, wrap it in plastic wrap, then refrigerate for 1 hour.

Meanwhile, to make the lemon curd, beat the whole eggs, yolks and sugar until well combined, then place in a small saucepan with the lemon juice and stir over low heat until the sugar dissolves. Add the butter and stir until the mixture is thick and smooth. Do not boil. Remove from the heat, then stir in the chocolate until smooth. Cool, then transfer the curd to an airtight container and refrigerate for 1 hour.

Preheat the oven to 180°C (350°F/Gas 4).

Roll out the pastry between two pieces of baking paper until 7 mm (⅜ inch) thick. Using a 5-cm (2-inch) biscuit cutter, cut out rounds and place on a baking tray lined with baking paper. Bake for 8-10 minutes, or until golden.

To assemble the verrines, arrange alternate layers of biscuit and lemon curd among the glasses. Garnish with glacé ginger before serving.

TIPS You can use ready-made butter shortbread biscuits if you don't have time to make the biscuits.

For a sweeter alternative, garnish the verrines with grilled meringue pieces instead of glacé ginger.

Banana milkshake with caramelised papaya and mango

Makes 6-8 large glasses

80 g (2¾ oz) caster (superfine) sugar

1 papaya, peeled, seeded and finely diced

1 large mango, peeled, stoned and finely diced

100 ml (3½ fl oz) pineapple juice

3 small gelatine leaves

1 banana

3 scoops vanilla ice cream

125 ml (4 fl oz/½ cup) milk

Heat the sugar in a frying pan over medium heat. As soon as it starts to caramelise, add the papaya and mango and stir to coat. Add the pineapple juice, then reduce the heat to low and cook for 7-8 minutes, or until the fruit has caramelised a little. Remove from the heat.

Soak the gelatine in cold water until soft, then drain and squeeze out the excess water. Add the gelatine to the fruit and combine well. Allow the fruit to cool completely, then divide evenly among the glasses and refrigerate for 1 hour.

Just before serving, peel and slice the banana and blend with the ice cream and milk until smooth.

To assemble the verrines, pour the milkshake over the fruit-filled glasses and serve immediately.

TIPS You can vary this recipe by replacing the vanilla ice cream with coconut ice cream and/or adding a dash of rum to the milkshake.

Another way to spice up the recipe is to add a touch of cinnamon or dust the verrine with unsweetened cocoa powder.

Christmas trees with Smarties

Makes 6–8 medium glasses

CHOCOLATE CREAM

200 ml (7 fl oz) milk

300 ml (10½ fl oz) pouring cream

7 egg yolks

70 g (2½ oz) caster (superfine) sugar

250 g (9 oz) dark chocolate, roughly chopped

CHOCOLATE TREE TOPPING

250 g (9 oz) dark chocolate, roughly chopped

6–8 ice-cream cones or 18–24 Gavotte (crisp, folded crepe) biscuits or ice-cream wafers

Smarties, whole or in pieces, to decorate

To make the chocolate cream, heat the milk and cream in a saucepan over medium heat to just below boiling point. Remove from the heat.

Whisk the egg yolks and sugar in a bowl, then pour onto the hot cream mixture, stirring continuously. Return the saucepan to the heat and stir over low heat with a wooden spoon until the mixture thickens enough to coat the back of the spoon. Remove from the heat. Add the dark chocolate and stir until smooth.

Fill the glasses with the chocolate cream (the diameter of the glasses needs to be slightly wider than the ice-cream cones). Refrigerate for at least 1 hour.

To make the topping, place the dark chocolate in a heatproof bowl over a saucepan of boiled water, making sure the base of the bowl does not touch the water. Allow to stand until the chocolate has melted.

Use a pastry brush to cover the cones or the Gavotte biscuits with chocolate (if you are using the biscuits, stick 3 biscuits together to make a pyramid). Stick on the Smarties, whole or in pieces, to decorate. Refrigerate for 5-10 minutes, or until the chocolate hardens, then carefully set the Christmas trees on top of the verrines just before serving.

Raspberry and pistachio tiramisu

Makes 6–8 large glasses

125 g (4½ oz/1 cup) fresh or thawed frozen raspberries, plus extra to decorate

30 g (1 oz) caster (superfine) sugar

18–24 savoiardi (sponge fingers), cut into small pieces

125 ml (4 fl oz/½ cup) amaretto liqueur

60 g (2¼ oz) pistachio nuts, crushed

4 chocolate biscuits (cookies), crushed

MASCARPONE CREAM

3 eggs, separated

50 g (1¾ oz) caster (superfine) sugar

250 g (9 oz) mascarpone cheese

Lightly crush the raspberries in a bowl with the sugar.

Arrange savoiardi biscuits on the bottom of the glasses, moisten with a drizzle of amaretto, then press down lightly with your fingertips. Add a layer of crushed raspberries, then place the glasses in the refrigerator.

To make the mascarpone cream, beat the egg yolks and half the sugar in a bowl until thick and pale. Then beat in the mascarpone cheese until smooth.

Whisk the egg whites until soft peaks form, then add the remaining sugar and beat until stiff peaks form. Gently fold into the mascarpone mixture.

To assemble the verrines, divide the mascarpone cream evenly among the glasses of savoiardi and crushed raspberries. Return to the refrigerator and chill for at least 2 hours.

Just before serving, lightly scatter crushed pistachios and chocolate biscuits over the verrines and garnish with a few raspberries.

Pear compote with chocolate shortbread biscuits

Makes 6–8 large glasses

CHOCOLATE SHORTBREAD

150 g (5½ oz) soft unsalted butter

110 g (3¾ oz) icing (confectioners') sugar

175 g (6 oz) plain (all-purpose) flour

3 tablespoons unsweetened cocoa powder

1 whole egg

1 egg yolk

PEAR COMPOTE

5 pears (such as williams or conference), peeled, cored and diced into large cubes

3 tablespoons honey

1 vanilla bean, split lengthways

To make the biscuit dough, heat the butter and sugar with electric beaters until pale and fluffy. Add the flour and cocoa and combine well. Add the whole egg and the yolk and combine well. Shape the dough into a disc, wrap it in plastic wrap, then refrigerate for 1 hour.

Meanwhile, to make the pear compote, place the pears in a medium saucepan. Add the honey, 3 tablespoons of water and split vanilla pod and cook over medium heat for 5–6 minutes. Remove from the heat. Allow to cool, then refrigerate for 1 hour. Remove the vanilla bean.

Preheat the oven to 180°C (350°F/Gas 4).

Roll out the biscuit dough on a lightly floured surface to 5 mm (¼ inch) thick. Cut out circles using a 6 cm (2½ inch) biscuit cutter or a glass. Place them on a baking tray lined with baking paper, and bake for 6–7 minutes, or until golden.

To assemble the verrines, fill the glasses with pear compote and top each verrine with a chocolate shortbread biscuit.

TIPS Use ready-made chocolate shortbread biscuits if you don't have time to make the biscuits.

If desired, reserve the top of the pears with the stems attached to garnish the verrines.

Champagne granita, strawberries and biscuits de Reims

Makes 6–8 large glasses

150 g (5½ oz) caster (superfine) sugar

750 ml (26 fl oz/3 cups) brut rosé Champagne

500 g (1 lb 2 oz) strawberries, hulled and diced

1 packet of roses de Reims biscuits (available from specialist food stores and select delicatessens), or savoiardi (sponge fingers)

To make the granita, heat the sugar and 150 ml (5 fl oz) of water in a small saucepan over low heat and stir until the sugar has dissolved. Bring to the boil, then remove from the heat and allow to cool. Add the Champagne and mix well, then pour into a wide, shallow container and freeze for at least 3 hours. Stir the granita mixture occasionally with a fork or a small whisk, working from the edges towards the centre to form ice crystals.

To assemble the verrines, arrange the strawberries in the bottom of the glasses. Crumble the biscuits into small pieces with your fingertips and cover the strawberries. Spoon the granita over the top and serve immediately.

Sweet verrines in a flash . . .

Fresh fruit choc-coated pretzel sticks with chocolate cream

Use Mikado chocolate sticks as skewers for fresh fruits and serve with chocolate sauce for dipping.

Lychees with coconut milk and ginger

Try lychees in syrup doused with coconut milk and topped with slices of pickled ginger: an original and simple Asian-style verrine.

Fresh curd cheese with black grapes and crème de cassis

There is nothing simpler than combining a fresh cheese with fruit. Here's an appetising idea: good-quality black grapes, fresh cheese and some crème de cassis poured over. After a heavy meal, this will go very easily with the end of a good bottle of red wine.

Cookies, vanilla custard and caramel

Create layers of vanilla custard, caramel and chocolate, separating each with a cookie. Cookies and cream are a wonderful match!

Marshmallow, fresh fruit and coulis

Fun and colourful! Brighten up a birthday or snack time for your young children with these appetising and vitamin-packed verrines: marshmallows, fresh fruits and a coulis.

Yoghurt, jam and muesli

A very familiar and popular dish at breakfast or brunch, this combination of dairy, fruit and grains, put together however you like, will be even more inviting assembled in an attractive verrine.

Oranges, cinnamon and shortbreads

An adaptation of the Moroccan-style orange soup: slices of peeled oranges, spiced with cinnamon, served with thin shortbread biscuits.

Surprise compotes

Combine a few different ready-made fruit compotes, each mixed with chocolate sprinkles, dried fruit or tiny sweets, by layering them in your verrines.

Fromage frais, chestnut purée and rolled wafers

Carefully combine the creaminess of fromage frais, the sweet chestnut purée from the Ardèche and delicate and crispy rolled wafers. You'll create a pretty verrine that's a guaranteed success.

Black forest brownie

A quick verrine, though a bit of a cheat: a scoopful of ready-made black forest cake, topped with cherries will be devoured quickly!

Iced coffee with amaretto

Indulge with a scoop of coffee ice cream, a very hot espresso, three drops of amaretto liqueur, some crumbled biscuits and chantilly cream . . .

Little baba-style madeleine cake

A madeleine sponge in the form of sweet baba, soaked in a mixture of fruit juice and rum.

Banana bounty

Slices of chocolate coated coconut confectionery and banana, then add coconut ice cream to make a banana split that rises above the ordinary!

Tagada cheese

Small pieces of *Fraises Tagada* (strawberry candy) in a fromage blanc with strawberry coulis. Childish? What of it . . . it's adored by all!

Anise-flavoured melon

Purée melon with a dash of pastis. This anise-flavoured gazpacho will invite itself to dessert.

Coffee mousse with nougat chips

Add crumbled nougat to ready-made coffee mousse for a very sweet treat.

Yoghurt, jam and muesli

Too often relegated to breakfast or Sunday brunch, this combination also makes an original dessert.

Harlequin-style fromage frais

An ultra-simple trifle will always delight young and old: fresh cheese with mango, kiwi fruit and strawberry.

index

Published in 2009 by Murdoch Books Pty Limited
First published by Marabout (Hachette Livre) as
Verrines 2006 and *Verrines toute fraîches* 2007

Murdoch Books Australia
Pier 8/9
23 Hickson Road
Millers Point NSW 2000
Phone: +61 (0) 2 8220 2000
Fax: +61 (0) 2 8220 2558
www.murdochbooks.com.au

Murdoch Books UK Limited
Erico House, 6th Floor
93-99 Upper Richmond Road
Putney, London SW15 2TG
Phone: +44 (0) 20 8785 5995
Fax: +44 (0) 20 8785 5985
www.murdochbooks.co.uk

Publisher: Jane Lawson
Editor: Sandra Loy
Designer: Katy Wall
Photographer: Akiko Ida
Production: Kita George

National Library of Australia Cataloguing-in-
Publication Data:
    Author: Maréchal, José.
    Title: Verrines / José Maréchal.
    ISBN: 9781741963663 (hbk.)
    Notes: Includes index.
    Subjects: Cookery, French – Appetisers – Desserts
    Dewey number: 641.5944

A catalogue record for this book is available from
the British Library.

Colour separation by Colour Chiefs.
Printed by 1010 Printing in 2009. PRINTED IN CHINA.

IMPORTANT: Those who might be at risk from the
effects of salmonella poisoning (the elderly, pregnant
women, young children and those suffering from
immune deficiency diseases) should consult their
doctor with any concerns about eating raw eggs.

OVEN GUIDE: You may find cooking times vary
depending on the oven you are using. For fan-forced
ovens, as a general rule, set the oven temperature
to 20°C (35°F) lower than indicated in the recipe.